Jeri,

Thank you for your support!

God bless!

EVERY
DAY
IS AN
INTERVIEW

MARIO McLEAN

Scripture taken from the New King James Version®. Copyright © 1982
by Thomas Nelson. Used by permission. All rights reserved.

This book is a work of non-fiction. Unless otherwise noted, the author and the publisher
make no explicit guarantees as to the accuracy of the information contained in this book
and in some cases, names of people and places have been altered to protect their privacy.

ISBN: 978-1-4834-7016-0 (sc)
ISBN: 978-1-4834-7015-3 (e)

Because of the dynamic nature of the Internet, any web addresses or links contained in
this book may have changed since publication and may no longer be valid. The views
expressed in this work are solely those of the author and do not necessarily reflect the
views of the publisher, and the publisher hereby disclaims any responsibility for them.

Any people depicted in stock imagery provided by Thinkstock are models,
and such images are being used for illustrative purposes only.
Certain stock imagery © Thinkstock.

Lulu Publishing Services rev. date: 07/14/2017

CONTENTS

OPENING PRAYER.. vii

ACKNOWLEDGEMENTS ix

PART ONE – I HAVE A STORY TO TELL....................................1

    CHAPTER 1 – AGAINST ALL ODDS 3

    CHAPTER 2 – GRADUATION DAY 9

    CHAPTER 3 – "WHAT'S YOUR 'WHY'?" 13

    CHAPTER 4 – TOUGH LOVE 15

    CHAPTER 5 – THE COUNTDOWN 23

    CHAPTER 6 – ARE YOU MY DADDY? 29

    CHAPTER 7 – #1 SECOND TO NONE 33

    CHAPTER 8 – WHO WILL? SPARTANS WILL!.............37

    CHAPTER 9 – CONCLUSION 43

PART TWO – KEYS TO SUCCESS 45

    1. DON'T THINK ABOUT IT. BE ABOUT IT!.................47

    2. NETWORK UNTIL YOU GET A NET WORTH 51

    3. LIGHT BULB MOMENTS 55

    4. WALK BY FAITH, NOT BY SIGHT 59

    5. GET COMFORTABLE BEING UNCOMFORTABLE .61

    6. KNOW YOUR WORTH 65

    7. DO YOU MEASURE UP? 69

    8. REFLECTION TIME..71

    9. FRIENDS – HOW MANY OF US HAVE THEM? 75

10. CHOOSE THE ROAD LESS TRAVELED 77

11. SET THE STICKY NOTE HIGH 81

12. EVERY DAY IS AN INTERVIEW....................................83

13. MENTORSHIP 89

CONCLUSION..93

CLOSING PRAYER 95

OPENING PRAYER

Dear Heavenly Father,

Thank you for allowing me to accomplish one of my biggest dreams, which since I was a little kid, was to write and publish my own book. Thank you for guiding my mind, my hands, and my will throughout the entire process. I know none of this would be possible without your help. With this book, I ask that you allow it to inspire others to also go after some of their biggest dreams too, whatever that may be. The story I have to tell, the situations I've been through and the experiences I have gained, have all impacted my life in a humbling way. I ask that you allow my story to make a positive difference in the lives of those that decide to read and/or take the time out of their day to hear about it. I ask that this book be the beginning to a new outlet in my personal life. I pray that it will open up more doors and opportunities that will allow for me to continue writing and telling my story to those who could benefit greatly from it. In your precious, glory and holy name I pray. Amen.

ACKNOWLEDGEMENTS

Thank you to Jesus Christ, my precious Lord and Savior. Thank you to my parents, Agatha McLean & Melvin Austin for giving birth to me. Though we didn't have the ideal family lifestyle growing up, I learned a lot from the both of you. You both taught me right from wrong. While it may not have been intentional, the experiences we went through have all shaped me into being the great man that I am today. And for that, I thank you!

Thank you to my beautiful fiancée, Amber Blanks, who continuously motivated me to write this novel and share my story. I'm extremely lucky to have a woman like you in my corner backing me up and encouraging me to reach my fullest potential.

Thank you to my two sisters, Mercedes & Melody for being there for me growing up. We shared many hard times and disappointments, but we made a way out of no way. I love you two dearly. Also, to my older siblings, Monique, Melvin and Marcus, thank you all for believing in me as well. I love each and every one of you!

Thank you to Helen and Mac Dashney. You two have been an amazing asset to my life. Helen, you really don't understand how much I appreciate all you have done for me. You are truly a blessing!

Lastly, to all of my family members, friends, co-workers, and anyone else that I may have missed, THANK YOU in advance for your support!

PART ONE

I HAVE A STORY TO TELL

CHAPTER 1

AGAINST ALL ODDS

It was my senior year and I had a few more months left to go before I graduated from one of the greatest universities in the world - Michigan State University. I was having an all-star senior year so far; I had my full-time job already locked and secured with Frito-Lay to be a District Sales Leader, my grades were great, and I was ready to finish achieving and accomplishing what many thought would be impossible for a young, African American male to do.

Before I graduated, there was one more personal goal that stood in my way. This was a goal I had set for myself a semester into my senior year – I wanted to be the student commencement speaker at graduation! Why? Well, why not? I wanted to challenge myself! It was that simple. For me, graduating wasn't enough. I considered my degree in Communication a bust, even though I had minored in Sales Communication as well. The reason being was because when I first came to MSU, I was a Marketing major and had dreams of getting into Eli Broad College of Business, but after failing Accounting twice and diminishing my business GPA, that dream was long gone.

You could see the type of person I was and honestly, the type of person I still am to this day; nothing was ever good enough for me. For someone else, graduating with a degree in anything, for all that matters is looked at as a huge accomplishment. But for me, I wanted more. Since I felt like I had let myself down by me not getting accepted into the business school, I had to prove to others that I still deserved to be in the business school one way or another. Being the student commencement speaker would show to the world that I had what it took to be mentioned in the same breath as other b-school students. While it probably wasn't even as big of a deal as I made the entire situation, this is how I truly felt deep down inside.

Whenever something didn't go the way I anticipated it going, that fueled me to go even stronger the next time around. I was never one to hang my head on any situation because at the end of the day, time waits for no man. So I had to be strong and keep it moving.

Months before auditions came, I can recall going into the business library numerous times to craft my speech. If I had an hour break in between classes, I was working on my speech passionately. When I first began to write my speech, I remember watching other student's speeches on YouTube. I immediately put an end to that because while watching their speeches, I realized that they all lacked one important thing – originality. Yes, some of them indeed had awesome speeches, but they were not as meaningful and sincere as the speech I pictured myself giving. Another thing I noticed that all the speakers did was read their speech word for word off of a sheet of paper for reference. Here's where I observed with a very critical eye. After I found out what the norm was or what everyone else was doing, I told myself, "Let's be different. Let's do something that has never been done before."

I knew exactly what needed to be done to set myself aside from the competition - Remember my speech word from word without having to read it from a paper, while still being confident and speaking directly from the heart.

Leading up to auditions, I felt extremely confident. I knew that NOBODY had a better speech than mine. Out of the hundreds of students in the school of Communication Arts and Sciences, it was only 7 of us who were actually brave enough to stick through with applying to be the student commencement speaker. I was the only African American student to apply and so of course, I quickly felt outnumbered. But I didn't let that affect me though. I still felt extremely confident in my speech, which I had worked on continuously for about 5 months straight.

After I had recited my speech with such passion and oozing confidence, I walked out the room knowing I was going to be the one delivering the speech on the big day. The judges had informed us all before we had auditioned that they would be emailing us with the winner that night. They also said that if we happen to have not been selected, they wouldn't discuss the results or give us any feedback. I remember thinking to myself, "Well, I'm not going to need any feedback because I already won." Looking back, I must say that I was both cocky and confident in my work.

After I left to go home, every 5 minutes, I'd refresh my email anxiously waiting for the results. Hours had gone passed and finally there was the email I was looking for with "Commencement Speaker" in the subject line. It read, "Hey Folks: I just wanted to let you know that the committee was unanimous in selecting Alan Printiss as the Commencement Speaker." My heart dropped. I was devastated. I truly felt robbed! At that moment, it felt like somebody had ripped my heart out and stomped on it a few times. All of the time I had spent in writing and rehearsing my speech, talking to my friends about how I was going to deliver an amazing speech on graduation day was over. I had failed myself.

All I could think about was the judges saying they wouldn't let us know why we didn't get selected in the event we weren't chosen to be the speaker. Although I did not know Alan, I was 100% sure his speech wasn't better than mine. I honestly wanted to hear his speech myself! I needed answers.

That next morning, much like I had done the night before, I kept refreshing my email, waiting for one of the judges to let me know what had happen and why I wasn't selected to be the speaker. At the very beginning when this was all a thought and a long shot, I knew the road was going to be tough. It's over 40,000 students that attend Michigan State – what made me think that for one second, they would have selected little ole me? But now that I actually had pursued my dream and had a chance, I took this defeat personal.

After about 100 refreshes later, I got the email I was searching for. It was one of the judges, who happened to be an Academic Advisor in the school of Com Arts. She reached out to me and said, "Hi Mario, I thought you did a great job last night. You should be very proud of yourself. I LOVED the message of your speech and think you should submit your speech to be the commencement speaker for the convocation (the 1 hour ceremony earlier in the day before our actual graduation ceremony)."

I remember thinking to myself, "If I just got denied to be the speaker at Com Arts graduation, how could you possibly think I would be able to be the speaker for the entire school?" And then it all made sense to me. God was testing my true character.

He wanted to see if I was going to let this defeat defer me from accomplishing my ultimate goal.

So like the Spartan in me, I put on my war clothes and got ready again to fight for what was mine. I made very minor tweaks to my speech before the new audition. I remember walking into the room ready to claim my reward. There were two judges in the room this time. Before I delivered my speech, they asked a few interview questions. I remembered them asking me "Why do you want to be the student commencement speaker?" The timing of this question could not have been more perfect. I responded, "I want to be the commencement speaker for two reasons: 1. I've been crafting this speech for the past 5 months and I really want my voice to be heard. I think it's the perfect way to end my undergraduate career here and 2. I had originally applied to be the speaker for the School of Com Arts but wasn't selected. And once you hear my speech, you'll see how I talk about why it's important to never give up the first time you don't achieve your goal. So I really just want to prove to myself that I have what it takes to do this."

After I gave my speech, the look on their faces was priceless. "You're the first person to give your speech without having to read it from a piece of paper. We are extremely impressed." I thanked them for their time and walked out the room feeling confident that off of that statement alone, I was going to be selected to be the student commencement speaker of Fall 2015!

On my way to Minnesota for a Spring Trip with my organization, the MSU Marketing Association, I was sitting in my seat on the bus and looking out the window. All of a sudden, I had received an email from the commencement committee and they had said that I had been selected to be the student commencement speaker for the convocation ceremony! My heart had dropped – I could have fainted; I was so damn excited! To go through the emotional roller coaster I went through of trying to accomplish this goal was all worth it in the end! I had finally taken what I deserved.

Persistence had paid off!

CHAPTER 2

GRADUATION DAY

It was May 8, 2015. I had just finished having brunch with President Simon and Bob Chapek, chairman of Walt Disney. The weather was fantastic. I couldn't have asked for a better day to graduate from college. Here I was, at Michigan State University, 21 years old, and about to do what only 3% of foster care children had done – which was graduate! And not only was I getting ready to graduate, I was about to deliver the commencement speech in front of thousands of people.

I kept on thinking that since I didn't want to read my speech off of a piece of paper that I would get up there and become nervous and forget my entire speech. I did not want to embarrass myself. These were all the thoughts that kept lingering in my head. I wanted to remove myself from the entire situation. I had allowed my nerves to completely take me out of my comfort zone.

About 40 minutes into the ceremony, my time was due. Here it was - I had 4 of my mentors in the audience, 2 who had flown in town just to see me, my family and hundreds of friends and classmates. I knew I couldn't let them down. Leading up to this moment, I probably had recited my speech over a hundred times. The night before, I remember waking up in the middle of the night multiple times to recite my speech. I had to make sure it was at the top of my mind.

So just like I had rehearsed, my speech had come out flawless. It was almost as if God was controlling my tongue and words were just coming out without me having to do anything. I remember grasping the audience attention from the very beginning of my speech all the way through. When I had finished, the standing ovation from the crowd was all the accreditation I needed to know that this was my calling.

And so as you can see, sometimes God allows for us to fail miserably at certain things. But ultimately, it's up to you to continue to keep pushing and take what's yours. For me, I wanted my story to be heard. I wanted to prove to myself that I had what it took to do the "impossible".

Something I found that was even more fulfilling is that MSU is now using my picture from speaking on stage that day to promote graduation week. My story/picture has appeared in the Lansing News, the annual President Letter that gets sent out to 500,000+ MSU Alumni, on the brochures in the cafeteria that sits on the lunch tables, in the Spartan Spirit Shop and on the Spartan Spirit Shop website!

Since giving my speech, other speaking opportunities have opened up for me as well. I was asked to come back to my middle school, Michigan Technical Academy, and be the guest Alumni Speaker at their 8th grade graduation ceremony. I also was granted the opportunity to be the Keynote Speaker at the 2016 Michigan Teen Conference at Eastern Michigan University, which is an annual conference consisting of foster care youth preparing for adult-living and planning for their future. Lastly,

I was selected into the National Foster Youth Institute Shadow Day Program. The NFYI Shadow Day program is a week long event that takes place in Washington, D.C., where foster care youth gets paired with their member of Congress and gain a better understanding of the legislative process and how they can use their personal experiences to create change in the child welfare system.

I think it is safe to say that I beat the odds that were set against me. Michigan State University was a thrillful ride to be a part of!

CHAPTER 3

"WHAT'S YOUR 'WHY'?"

I know a lot of you are probably thinking, "Where did you get this motivation and determination from?" As famous author, speaker and hip hop preacher, Eric Thomas, would say "What's your 'why'? Why do you do what you do with a passion?" My 'why' was I knew what it was like to be homeless – what it was like to have NOTHING. And so in me knowing that, failure was not an option. It just wasn't. I always prided myself on being 10 steps ahead of the competition. The way my life was handed to me, I had already failed once by default. There was no way I was going to let myself fail again while on my own watch. So if you will, please allow for me to tell you my story on where I got my self-motivation and determination from.

> "A successful man is one who can lay a firm foundation
> with the bricks others have thrown at him"
> —David Brinkley

As an African American male growing up in Detroit, MI, life wasn't easy, to say the least. At the age of 6, my two older sisters and I were each placed in the foster care system because both of our parents abused drugs and alcohol and we had no stable home life. Although I was young, I can still vividly remember some of the struggles we faced as a family. I remember going to sleep in one place and opening my eyes and I'd be over someone else's house or even in a shelter. As time passed, and my parents' addiction grew, my foundation for wanting so much more out of my own life also grew at a rapid rate.

When we had to live at a shelter for a period of time, I knew my parents could no longer afford to take care of us. It was awful living at a shelter – you are living with people off the streets, the food is disgusting, the beds are hard and filthy, etc. For me, the worst part was going to school and having to act like I was living a "normal" life back at home. Meanwhile, my life was all but "normal". I remember kept asking God "why?" "Why did he choose me and my family to go through this situation? What did I do to deserve this?" I kept questioning God, searching for answers. The funny thing about God is that whenever we ask him a question we want the answers right then and there. But he makes us wait for it and humbles us in the process. But later on, we end up finding the true reason why God did the things he did or allowed for us to experience the things we experienced.

I'd like to think of this time period in my life as my "character-defining" years. I really had to find out what my purpose in life was and what exactly God put me on this earth to do. At the time I didn't know, but I knew that staying in shelters was not the life I wanted to continue to live. It was at this time when I had found my purpose in life and my 'why'.

CHAPTER 4

TOUGH LOVE

On about 3/1/2000, Protective Services received
a referral with allegations of physical neglect
in regards to the McLean children –Mercedes
McLean (11 years old), Melody McLean (10
years old) & Mario McLean (6 years old).

To the best of my knowledge, the day my two older sisters and I went into the foster care system, Child Protective Services had got in contact with my mom and dad and they pretty much told them that they wanted to help us out. Come to find out, this turned out to be a scheme to get us down there without them having to come look for us. My parents just needed to bring us to their office. When we had arrived there, they had told my mom and dad "Thanks for bringing the kids in, you can leave now." My mom was in complete disarray. She said, "I thought y'all were going to help us! If I would've known y'all were going to be taking my kids, I would've never brought them down here in the first place!"

After all that commotion went on, and my mom and dad finally calmed down and came to the realization that this was the safest place for us to be at the time, Mercedes, Mel & I each went to the back room where they had gave us some teddy bears to play with until they figured out our placements.

I remember having mixed thoughts and emotions once I found out that I would no longer be with my family on a day-to-day basis. A part of me was scared because at the time, I wasn't too sure of the entire picture. Was this going to be a temporary process? Was this only going to be for a couple days? A couple months? A couple years? I literally had no clue of what was going on. My main concern was to at least be kept with my sisters; I felt like I would be able to get through anything as long as I had them.

On the other hand, I envisioned this being a great opportunity for me and my sisters. I mean we had seen a lot at such early age. We witnessed the drugs and alcohol, the fighting and the arguments between my mom and dad, and the homelessness. Anybody willing to accept us with open arms after we went through the parent neglect we were going through, we had no choice but to be grateful. Our lives were not heading in the right direction, so maybe change was exactly what we needed to turn our lives back around.

Melody and Mercedes ended up being placed in the same home while I unfortunately, got split up. My first foster home I went to was with a nice, older couple, Carrie and "Smitty". Carrie and Smitty also had another foster child named Steve. I remember walking into their house for the first time feeling so out of place. I was extremely scared. I didn't know who these people were and they just welcomed me into their home. I was so young and confused. I walked straight to my room; clutching and squeezing my teddy bear that the agency had given me, which now seemed to be my best friend at the moment.

Steve's bed was next to mine. I can't quite remember the conversation Steve and I had when we first met. The only thing I remember was crying! I mean I cried 24/7. I thought I would never see my family again. I didn't eat. I couldn't sleep. I just wanted to be with my family despite everything we were dealing with at the time. I loved my parents dearly, but them placing us in the middle of this difficult situation was going to make it hard for me to really be able to love them wholeheartedly again.

It was at this moment, when I began to look at my parents differently. I began to grow hate towards them because if it wasn't for their selfish ways, their refusal to stop abusing drugs and alcohol, we wouldn't even be in this situation in the first place! It was at this moment when I realized that all I had was myself. I wiped every single tear from my face that night and "grew up".

Six years old is when I truly believe I gained the spirit of self-motivation. I knew that if I wanted anything, I would have to go out and get it myself. From that day forward, I stopped depending on others to do anything for me. I removed all my hopes in human beings and counted anything given to me as extra or an added benefit. I didn't know how I would arise from this situation. I didn't know what to expect. I knew that as long as I had me though, I would be in good hands.

After being in foster care for about 3 weeks, Melody had moved in with Carrie, Smitty, Steve and I. I was extremely happy! My eating habits changed – I started eating a little bit more than I did when I first had moved in. I felt more comfortable being in foster care with at least one of my sisters.

Then after a while, we found out we could start seeing our

entire family once a week on Thursday's. I honestly didn't know how I would react to seeing my mom and dad for the first time since entering the system. I thought I would be sad and closed, but it turned out I was the exact opposite. I was awfully ecstatic to have my family together again. We played games, we talked and we caught up. Throughout this process, my parents became very unpredictable though. Sometimes they show up to the "visits", sometimes they wouldn't. Sometimes we would have great meetings, sometimes we wouldn't. We laughed and we cried. These mixtures of emotions and behaviors my parents were displaying to my sisters and I made me realize that they really had a problem that was so much bigger than them. They were being controlled by the drugs and the alcohol so much that they never stopped to realize for once the effect this entire situation had on us. It was almost as if the drugs were psyching them out, making them think they were being great parents when in reality, they weren't. Though my sisters and I smiled and had a great time at the visits, deep down inside we were broken.

During this process, I had a ton of questions – was it something I did or said? Was it something my sisters did or said to make us end up in this predicament?

The more serious question though was when were we going to get out of the system? I could tell from my parents, mainly my moms' sporadic visits with us on our scheduled days, that it wasn't going to be anytime soon.

I'd like to think from my mom's point of view that she had become content and "free". She could still remain doing whatever it was that she wanted to do because her responsibility of taking care of her kids was removed from her. Because of this, she figured that whether she did good or bad, at least her kids were in good hands. This to me didn't necessarily make any sense. I would have thought it would've been the exact opposite. Us being taken away should have opened up her eyes and made her understand that this is serious business. This should have showed her that her rights can be taken away from her and that we would have been another statistic in the foster care system. But no, since we were in a stable environment, this only excited her even more to continue living her lifestyle carefree.

When you are dealing with an addiction however, common sense somehow is no longer common. It becomes tough for you to break certain habits because your mental is completely overruled by your wicked ways. You become insane because you continue to do the same things that got you in the position you are currently in and expect a different result every time.

Besides the alcohol and the drugs, my mom was struggling with a lot – she had been diagnosed with a Depressive Disorder, my brother who would've been 2 years older than me, Michael, had died of crib death, etc. So to her defense, I understand completely. There was a lot going on at the time and it became hard to juggle the amount of stresses that were placed on her life at the moment.

On the other hand, my dad was the exact same way. He too, allowed the drugs and alcohol to continue to control his actions and behaviors. However, what separated my dad from my mom was he was able to overcome his addiction. Also, I feel that my dad showed more effort and diligence with the system to try to get me and my sisters out. While it took him many years to do so, what was important was that he never gave up and kept fighting. He was able to cope with the many struggles he was facing and overcome his circumstances for the greater good of our family. When it came to our family visits, my dad was always there to see how things were going with us. Like my mom, he too, missed some visits, but he managed to make it to more than she did.

About a year living with Carrie and Smitty, they had to leave town because Carrie's sister was getting pretty sick and she needed to take care of her. She wanted to bring Mel & I with her but after my dad refused, we were placed with another foster care mother by the name of Charlene.

Charlene had a house full of kids – She had two biological children, Bre' Onna and Matthew. One adopted son, Tyson, both Mel and I, and three other foster kids, Trayshawn, Diamond and Shawnetta. Then after some time, Mercedes ended up coming to live with us too!

Mel and Mercedes foster care home experiences were not as pleasant as mine starting off. Their very first foster home, their foster mother locked them in the basement and starved them for days. Then they were placed in an all-girl group home where they experienced many more unpleasant experiences. So for them to go through all of that and finally be in a foster home where the love was genuine, was fulfilling for me because I knew that we all had each other and we were safe.

Charlene was a great mother to us! She was amazing in the kitchen – we had huge meals every night. For school, we had bagged lunches packed to the max with all types of goodies from Sam's Club and Costco. I was living the dream. For the first time, I felt comfortable to pull my lunch box out at the lunch table without being embarrassed for what I had brought to school.

Charlene truly cared for my family. She made my view on foster care change drastically because she went through so much to put a smile on every single one of her kids' faces, whether they were biological, adopted or foster kids. A big mistake I made as a kid was I would compare Charlene to my real parents. I would always wonder why she would go out of her way to do things for Mercedes, Mel & I but my parents wouldn't do the same.

As I grew older, I realized that this wasn't a valid argument because my parents were not in any way, shape or form able to provide for us at the time. They had to work on themselves first before they could help anybody.

CHAPTER 5

THE COUNTDOWN

The agreement to regain custody of us was clear cut and dry. My parents had to drop weekly/random drug screens as requested, had to attend Narcotics Anonymous/Alcohol Anonymous meetings regularly, complete a 90 treatment program and most importantly, secure housing and be able to have a job with steady income to pay rent.

Court ordered treatment plan for Agatha McLean:

Substance Abuse
- Submit weekly random drug/alcohol screens within 24 hours of request and under conditions as ordered by the Court.
- Out-patient substance abuse treatment
- After-care as recommended by the treatment facility
- NA/AA meetings twice a week

Counseling/Therapy
- Individual therapy

- Family therapy
- Mental health treatment consistent with diagnosed condition, including medication if recommended

Parenting time
- Weekly supervised parenting time at the agency

Court ordered treatment plan for Melvin Austin:

Substance abuse
- Submit weekly random drug/alcohol screens within 24 hours of request and under conditions as ordered by the court
- Out-patient substance abuse treatment
- After-care as recommended by the treatment facility
- NA/AA meetings twice a week

Parenting time
- Unsupervised parenting time at foster care workers discretion and if parent is in full compliance with treatment plan

Both parents were supposed to do the following:

- Maintain suitable housing
- Maintain a legal source of income
- Fully cooperate with the Family Independence Agency
- Attend all court hearings

Between the years 2000-2002, my parents had made little to no improvement since we were placed in the system. My mom had not been able to invest in substance abuse treatment over that span. She still had not demonstrated that she was able to remain free from using substances. In addition, it always appeared that she was in total denial of what impact her substance abuse had had on our family.

My dad on the other hand, appeared to take his court involvement somewhat more seriously. However, he too, had had difficulty remaining drug free. Apparently, they both had been made aware that failure to provide negative urine screens consistently could result in a Permanency Custody Petition being initiated.

With Mel, Mercedes and I being in foster care for two years, our parents still had not been able to secure adequate housing for themselves, let alone for us. My dad, although employed, didn't even meet the requirements as set down by the agency and the court. It was noted that progress for us to be able to return back to either one of them at the time was poor, at best.

I remember my sisters and I getting more and more frustrated as time grew over the years and our parent's progress remained the same. We ended up having to take individual therapy sessions to help cope with our feelings.

Mercedes anger was a little more outspoken than the way Mel and I felt. She even expressed at one point she did not wish to attend visits with mom and dad any longer, as she was tired of them not doing what they were supposed to do, except for visitations. Since Mercedes was the oldest, it was easy for Mel and I to pretty much feel the same way. It hurt us seeing our big sister dealing with the situation the way she did because we were expecting her to be the strong one out of the group.

In hindsight, therapy really didn't work for me because I was never one to voice my opinions. I always kept my feelings bottled up because I didn't want anybody to think I was a charity case. I liked dealing with things quietly and on my own. When my mom and dad would miss visits, I'd display an enormous amount of sadness, as I would cry for hours the evenings in which when they would miss. I couldn't be seen like this. A man wasn't supposed to cry right?

The longer we stayed in foster care, it was like the worse my parents got. I had seen with my own two eyes that you literally had to hit rock bottom before you could start seeing progress again. I can recall one time my mom had some guy pick her up from one of the visits and my dad assaulted both him and her for coming up there. While my dad intentions may have been right, as he didn't want us to be around any random men, his actions portrayed differently and he made the agency look at him with a more critical eye.

I think that incident though, made him buckle down and begin working harder on his treatment plan to get me and my sisters out of the system. He quickly began showing progress, although he indeed relapsed a few months into his first rehab treatment. However, he was honest about it and got right back on track.

What held my dad up in the process was trying to find employment and suitable housing. Our case worker advised him to defer these two goals until he finished his 90 day treatment program. Once he completed his 90 day treatment program, he gained full-time employment at KFC, where he made about $400-500 weekly. However, three quarters of his pay went towards back child support he owed, as it was automatically being deducted from his paycheck. Because of this, it was hard for him to keep his head above water.

It wasn't until he finished his treatment plan that the court ordered when he was able to get involved in the Project

Infinity Program at Travelers Aid Society of Metro Detroit. This program assisted him with housing and casement services so that he could now become a productive member of society. The program allowed clients to become home owners within two years, if they had demonstrated they were able to afford rental property. Just like his first rehab treatment program, Travelers Aid was a drug free program that offered random drug screens and other case management services as well.

While my dad continued to make progress, my mom status on her treatment plan stayed the same. She mentioned to our case worker that her goals were to "get my stuff together, do everything possible, and loving my kids". Her words however, spoke much louder than her actions. She stopped doing drug/alcohol screens, got kicked out of her treatment center due to lack of absence, etc.

About 4 years into the foster care system, Mercedes, Mel & I went on to live with my Aunt Pam, my dad's sister, until he was able to secure housing through Section 8.

CHAPTER 6

ARE YOU MY DADDY?

On October 21, 2005, it was ordered by the court that sole legal and physical custody had been granted to my dad and that our case was terminated! Reasonable efforts by my dad had been made to preserve and unify our family once again.

By the time my dad had gotten us out of the foster care system, I was about 12 years old and on my way to middle school. I found it quite comical how my dad tried to pretty much pick off where he left off at before we had went into the system. Yes, of course, I was happy to be out of the system but I felt like he owed us a huge apology. Though my dad did sit us down at the table the day we finally moved into our own house, and apologized for everything we had been through over the past 5 years, I still needed and wanted more from him.

As time grew, I was starting to see that my dad still couldn't really afford to take care of us. A lot of it was lack of will not skill. My dad had got through the drug and alcohol addiction, but now another addiction grew – gambling. Not only was his gambling addiction beginning to ruin our family again, he had begun dating a woman he met during his treatment program and she had eventually moved in with us. This was a huge mistake on his behalf for a number of reasons. One, his counselor told him not to jump into a relationship at the time because he still needed to get his life together and be able to provide for his kids. Secondly, she mentioned to him the simple fact that "What if she didn't like the kids?"

Undoubtfully so, this is exactly what happened. Once his girlfriend moved in with us, she wanted to be first. This again, was contradicting from my sisters and I point of view because we had been placed on the back burner mainly our whole lives. And then here comes this random lady out of nowhere who begins demanding more attention than us. We needed answers. My dad went on to marry her but after their marriage lasted only a few months, he came to the conclusion that this wasn't a smart decision and that he needed to get his priorities straight yet again. They then separated and parted ways.

I like to think that my dad thought parenting was a one-time thing. What I mean by this is that he thought the minute he accomplished something or did something that would benefit us, then his job was done. He thought that getting us out of the foster care system was enough. What he failed to realize is that that was just the beginning. The real work would begin after we were back in his custody.

So back to my point - parenting is definitely an on-going process. It was then when my dad admitted that he did not have the parenting skills needed to take care of our family. We began going to family counseling so that my dad could get more help in raising us.

In the midst of all this going on, exactly how I did when I was in foster care, I continued to focus on my education and not lose sight of my ultimate goal. My goal was to let my education pave the way for me. With me overcoming foster care and still being able to obtain a 3.5 g.p.a throughout elementary and now middle school, I just needed to do the same, if not better, so that I could have the same results in high school and then college!

CHAPTER 7

#1 SECOND TO NONE

In 2007, I had got accepted into Cass Technical High School. I met some of my dearest friends, many in which I am still heavily connected with today. Cass Tech wasn't just an ordinary high school, it was like a family. We joked, we played, but at the end of the day, we all were there for the well-being of our education.

Throughout my time at Cass, I was a very active and engaged student. I was heavily involved in numerous student organizations such as Business Professionals of America (BPA), Michigan Ross School of Business Enriching Academics in Collaboration with High Schools (MREACH), Academic Games, etc. I also had won Homecoming Prince & Prom King.

One thing that made my experience at Cass memorable though was meeting my high school sweetheart – Amber Blanks.

Amber and I never had a class together, other than 5th hour lunch. Since we sat on opposite sides of the room, it was easy for me to spot her beauty from a distance. I remember at the time I tried to talk to her, she mentioned to me that she had a boyfriend. So I waited until they had broken up to fall in line.

It was weird when we first hooked up. I had caught her in

the lunchroom and I said to her "So when are we going to go together?" She replied, "Now." I didn't think she was serious, but I took that as my cue to make things official.

I can recall the beginning stages of our relationship being very rocky. Since my dad was paying my phone bill at the time, my phone stayed off due to his inability to stop gambling and take care of the bills. On the weekends, Amber and I barely talked and if we did, I was either using one of my cousin's or someone else's cell phone. And if that wasn't the case, we would simply chat via Facebook.

But when we did talk, the conversations were magical. I still remember the first time we talked on the phone until the sun had rose. We talked about everything; life goals, favorite colors (you know.. the usual for first timers). But the thing that I feel made Amber much more attracted to me was when I told her about my experiences in foster care. She had no clue what I had been through. And I think the fact that I'm always smiling no matter the situation is what people like about me the most.

Whenever my phone bill was paid, we would fall asleep on the phone every night. It instantly became one of our rituals. Even throughout college, we still fell asleep on the phone nearly every night - given our schedule permitting. One thing I will say that kept Amber and I relationship so well-knit together definitely was our communication. There was never a gap or disconnect. In fact, almost everything about our relationship was too "perfect".

We never argued and if we did, it was either about something petty or we both just said "Let's just forget about it and move on." This may not have been the best way to go about certain situations but for us, it worked.

Amber was so smart and intelligent! She pushed me to be

a better person. And in return, I made sure I pushed her to be an even better person than I was. Whether it was through certain achievements or awards, it was like we would each be in competition with one another. Amber and I are very goal-oriented people. I think for us, accomplishing goals is what motivates us the most.

I found it rather easy to love Amber because it's genuinely in my spirit. I come from a background where I didn't get much love and support from the people I needed it from most. So because of that, I know what it takes to make others feel happy because I've been longing for that feeling my entire life!

You can ask any of my friends – I started off our relationship with the big guns. Expensive gifts, unexpected surprises, you name it, I was doing it. I knew what it was like to be the "perfect boyfriend". I knew that if I started off big in the relationship then I would have to be consistent and constantly improve. I pretty much fed off of my own energy and set the bar high early on into our relationship.

CHAPTER 8

WHO WILL? SPARTANS WILL!

When it was time to go off to college, a lot of people were predicting us to break up. I guess winning class couple didn't mean anything huh? We would be attending rival schools, as she was going to University of Michigan - Ann Arbor and I was going to Michigan State. But much like it was when I was growing up, I ignored what people thought and continued being and doing me. I knew that I wasn't going to find another "Amber" so I had to straighten up and get with the "program".

I didn't know how I was going to afford it, but I knew I was going to college! My dad didn't have a dime saved up. If it was up to him to put me through school, I was screwed. However, that didn't deter me from still following through and pursuing my dreams. My goal was to definitely document in my personal statement my financial needs and circumstances and somehow a miracle would happen.

I got accepted into Michigan State University with a few scholarships and a ton of loans. I'll be the first to tell you, I had no issue in taking out loans if it was for a good cause. Especially given the position I was in, I had no choice.

I deeply understood that I had no room for error in college.

So from day one, I made a promise to myself that I would grind it out despite my financial hardships and every other odd that was set out against me. My goal was to be out of MSU in 4 years with a well-paying full-time job.

I found the transition from high school to college to be rather smooth, with little to no resistance. I personally think those who have a tough time transitioning from high school to college struggle because it's their first glimpse of independence. If you looked at my life, I had pretty much been independent since I was 6, so nothing was new to me really.

One of the challenges I dealt with early on in college though, was each semester when it was time to figure out how I was going to pay for it. Again, I didn't have any scholarship money so I was taking out numerous loans. In fact, I had reached the maximum limit of loans I could take out in my name and had to depend on my parents to get approved for a Parent Plus Loan. Well, I knew my mom didn't have any established credit history and a plethora of random jobs, where she only worked for a few months, so that wasn't going to work. On the other hand, my dad had a job but his credit history was terrible!

I'll never forget the conversation we had when I told him I needed him to take out a loan in his name so that I can continue going to school. He made it seem like it was my fault for going to college. He didn't want to be responsible for paying loans that really wasn't benefiting him. All I could think was "Your credit is already messed up. I rather continue messing yours up than to hurt mine before I even start my career." But I kept my mouth closed. I kept on pushing. I knew God would make a way out of no way.

My dad would go on to apply for the Parent Plus Loan and get declined every semester due to his credit history. This caused us to have to appeal their decision EVERY single semester. And I don't know how, but we would always get approved the second time around.

Throughout my time at MSU, I networked with thousands of students and many faculty members. Michigan State was my home away from a home I never even had. I believe what makes any University great would definitely have to be its people. MSU had some of the most welcoming and loving people I had ever met.

A connection I hold near and dear to my heart was one I made my freshman year with my BUS 101 Professor, Helen Dashney. Helen noticed how I was always the first one to turn in my assignments, participate in classroom discussions, etc. At the end of the school year on the last day of class, she pulled me to the side and said "If you ever need anything or simply would like to stay in touch, please reach out to me." One of my greatest strengths has always been recognizing opportunities and leveraging resources. Whenever an opportunity is made available to me and I see a benefit in it, it's almost as if a light bulb goes off in my head and I make sure I take advantage of it.

Till this day, Helen and I remain very close friends. While she would say I did all of the work, she is a big part of my successes while at MSU. She was behind the scenes coaching me and making sure I was ready for whatever came my way. She introduced me to some key individuals throughout her personal network, which allowed for me to leverage them as well.

The point I'm getting to is find someone who truly believes in you and genuinely want to see you have a better life than the one in which you were handed. My situation was different – I had told Helen what I had been through and somehow she was able to fill that void as a mother that had been left open for a very long time.

I remember when I first thought about applying to be the student commencement speaker, I made sure I checked in with Helen to get her thoughts. When she told me that she knew I could do it, that little boost of confidence was literally all I needed to know that I indeed, could do it.

The biggest success at Michigan State was after I graduated, Helen and her husband, Mac, decided to create an Endowment Fund in my name at MSU! It was their way of recognizing me and passing my approach to success forward.

Mac and Helen Dashney are both Michigan State University graduates and have been active supporters of the university for more than 30 years. Mac and Helen have both dedicated a large portion of their careers to the education of students, at Michigan State University as well as in the public school system in Michigan. In Helen's tenure at the Eli Broad College of Business, she has advised countless MBA and undergraduate students in her roles as director of MBA Career Services and the Financial Market Institute.

This scholarship is given by the Dashneys in honor of Mario McLean, a 2015 alumnus of Michigan State University. A native of Detroit, MI, Mario spent several years of his childhood in the foster care system, in which he learned to take responsibility for himself at a very young age. Understanding that a college education would be necessary if he were to rise above his circumstances, he enrolled in MSU where he studied communication with a specialization in sales.

Nothing came easy for Mario, but through hard work, good time management, unwavering determination and an extraordinarily positive attitude, Mario completed his studies in four years, capping his graduation by delivering the student speech at the University Convocation. Privileged to know Mario from the start of his freshman year, we establish this scholarship in his honor with the hope of lightening the financial burden of students as determined to succeed as Mario.

I couldn't express my gratitude enough for such an honor! This was literally the best thing that has ever happened to me. Knowing that someone can limit their loans and use my scholarship as a way to help with their financial load is so rewarding. The fact that this will continue forever is still beyond me!

CHAPTER 9

CONCLUSION

No matter what you've been through or are currently going through, you can overcome! You have to grab hold of your life. Be accountable. Stop looking for excuses and people to blame for your life being a certain way. Acknowledge the situation, come up with a game plan and execute. It's that's simple. Nothing in life is easy – I'll be the first person to vouch for that. However, what is easy is to do absolutely nothing. It's easy to point the finger at somebody. Why not make a change or be the change that you want to see? Yes, change is going to take some sleepless night and quite a few failures. But at the end of the day, those sleepless nights and failures are all going to be worth it in the end.

You can't allow the Alan Printiss's of the world to stop your shine! If you want something, go after it. As long as you continue to move toward your goal and not run from it, you'll become a better person today than you were yesterday! And if you're lucky, you'll find someone like Helen who'll complete the missing pieces to your puzzle.

I hope that this short autobiography on my life gave you some motivation to let you know that you can do whatever it is you put your mind to. You just have to have the will and the mindset to do so!

PART TWO

KEYS TO SUCCESS

KEY #1

DON'T THINK ABOUT IT.
BE ABOUT IT!

N ow I know this may sound crazy, but too many times I've witnessed people wanting something near and dear to their hearts but, unfortunately, allowed themselves to get too caught up in the thinking process that they never even achieved their goals. I'm not saying that you should go do something drastic that involves a major life change without giving it some thought; I'm saying if it's something you really want, don't think too much on it, just do it.

Example: Since I was a kid who had been through many obstacles, most in which your average kid wouldn't have been through, and still managed to make it out - I wanted to tell my story. I always knew I wanted to write a novel on my life. It was one of those long-term goals that I just had to cross off of my bucket list. As I grew older and finished school and began working full-time, I realized a few things: 1. I was in a position in my life where my long term goal was now a short term goal. However, I would always find an excuse not to start working on it. When I got home and it would be time to start writing my book, I would say things like "I'm too tired." Or "I really don't feel like doing anything productive right now. I just want to relax." And 2. One thing I began noticing quickly was while I dreadfully made excuses, time was passing me by and I still hadn't accomplished my dream of writing a book. I was thinking way too much!

So I had to start being proactive and begin taking it one step at a time. Instead of trying to write the entire book in one sitting, I began dedicating a certain number of hours per day or even per week until it was finished. For those who may not know, writing a book can be a very challenging thing to do. You began having writers block, start wondering how much it's going to cost to edit your book and/or publish it, or you may even talk yourself out of the entire situation completely - thinking it's not even capable or attainable, but in all actuality, it is!

If this situation sounds familiar to you then you are thinking way too much! You need to just do it! If you really want that new car and have never had to pay a car note before, just do it! If you really want a house and are tired of wasting your money on renting apartments, just do it! Worry about the expenses part later (I mean if it's not feasible for you then, of course, don't set yourself up for failure right out of the gate, but I mean if it is feasible and you are just overthinking the entire situation, go ahead and do it). At the end of the day, if it's something you really want, treat yourself! I'm big on personal happiness! If you can honestly agree with the decision of purchasing something or doing something that is going to make you feel exuberant afterwards, I certainly recommend taking the steps to do so.

Go with whatever situation is going to make you feel good deep down inside. If you feel it in your gut and your heart, 9/10 this is something you really think will make you extremely happy after doing! It has been shown that these two feelings have not been known to disappoint. The feeling of getting something that you've always dreamed of is a feeling that can't be explained.

As you get closer to your goals and begin seeing short term results, your effort escalates because you now are a believer that dreams do come true. Once you begin noticing small changes, you become that more determined to find out even bigger results. Soon you'll get to the point where you don't think any more about the end result because you trust and believe in the process.

Moral of the story is to make yourself happy! Take that first step of simply putting forth the initial attempt of doing whatever it is that you would like to do and just watch life take its course! What I don't want you to do is get so caught up in the thinking process, the 'what if' or what could potentially happen, that you allow it to psyche you out of going after what you really want. Don't think about it. Be about it.

KEY #2

NETWORK UNTIL YOU GET A NET WORTH

This could be something as simple as going to college. By doing this, you already are granted with the platform that you need that provides you access to thousands of individuals from various backgrounds and cultures. From there, take a moment to spend some time with those individuals and find out both the differences and similarities that you each might share. After that, the ball is in your court for you to score on any opportunities that presents itself. Or if the opportunity isn't there, connect the dots and create one!

For example, if you plan on being a doctor and you just so happen to have a friend whose parent is already a doctor, take the time to introduce yourself to that individual. Find out what exactly he/she did to get them to where they are today. What were some key jobs and/or experiences they have had that gave them the skill set to be successful in their field? Get their contact info and follow-up.

LinkedIn

If you don't have one already, I would highly recommend that you create a LinkedIn profile. LinkedIn is basically the professional version of Facebook. You create a profile; fill out your experiences, previous job history, awards, etc. You literally can copy and paste from your resume and you're already on a good path to having a decent LinkedIn profile page.

In fact, LinkedIn is better than a resume because you can put more experiences on there that you may have had to take off of your resume due to the 1 page limit. Once you've created a LinkedIn profile and added in all of your experiences, now you just need to connect with people you may or may not already know. You can even search by specific companies and find people who already work there and then connect and reach out to them that way as well. Do you see how making the connection with someone and following back up with them can set you aside from the person who just connected with them but never followed back up or reached out to them? Who do you think is more likely to get the job? The person who connected and also followed back up is more likely going to be the one to get the job.

Remember: It's not about who you know. It's about what you do with the people you know. And to take it one step further, LinkedIn gives you the opportunity to make yourself stand out from the crowd and appeal to recruiters. All it takes is for you to put in the time to make your profile an "All-Star".

This is done first by having a professional headshot for your profile picture. I can't stress this enough. I see a lot of people that have cropped out pictures of when they were dressed up for prom, graduation pictures with their cap still on, etc. and it's just not professional. Make the investment to get a cheap J.C. Penny headshot done or even if you know a friend who has their own camera, see if they will do it to help cut cost. It definitely pays off in the long run.

Once the profile picture is clear and professional with a white background, next is the tag line that goes directly under your name. I've seen it all from standard job positions such as "Manager, Student, Accountant, etc." to "Highly skilled professional seeking career opportunities in..." Which one do you think sounds more attractive? Well, it really depends on your purpose. If you are someone who is looking for recruiters to reach out to you then having a long tag line may work best for your particular situation. But if you are pretty set in your current role and no longer seeking recruiter's attention then something more standard will get the job done for you.

The bio section on LinkedIn is also important because it shows your personal attributes, your interests, and your character – all things that aren't necessarily on your resume but are equally important to recruiters.

Next is the education and work experience section. I pretty much covered this in the opening – simply copy and paste this information from your resume. This is the easiest way to do it. You want your education and work experience to be listed in reverse chronological order (most recent at the top). Another thing that will get your LinkedIn profile to stand out is if you add logos next to your job or education experience. If someone is scrolling down your page and not really reading and they see a logo that they recognize or used to work for, etc., they are more likely to either connect with you because you now have something in common or they will simply stop and read through your profile to see all that you have to offer.

Another thing that is pretty cool about LinkedIn is you can

add links to your education and work experience. For example, on my page I have that I was the commencement speaker at MSU Class of 2015 graduation ceremony, and right under that is the link for someone to watch it, if interested. Adding links adds a lot of credibility to your profile because it's physically showing what you've said you've done in writing.

Having 500+ connections on LinkedIn is another easy way to make your profile shine bright like a diamond. I wouldn't recommend just connecting with hundreds of people you don't know just to reach 500+ connections. If you go this route, you risk losing credibility if you're connected with someone and one of your other connections wants you to connect them to him/her and you don't know them personally. You then serve no benefit because you wouldn't be able to formally introduce them to each other. That's why it's important for you to take the time to get to know people offline so that online the dots connect perfectly.

Lastly, there are other cool things you can do on LinkedIn to make your profile reach "All-Star" status, such as request or write a recommendation on someone's profile, endorse someone for their skills, write a blog, etc. The key is the more you put into your profile, the more you'll get out of it. I can't even count how many times I've had recruiters reach out to me in regards to high paying job opportunities, etc. and all I did was decorate my profile.

This is why when people say "There's no jobs out there." or "I can't find a job." I say to myself that they haven't put in the work. There's thousands of opportunities out here, you just have to work on yourself first and then know how to market yourself to the right audience!

Begin with LinkedIn and network until you get a net worth!

KEY #3

LIGHT BULB MOMENTS

Whenever I spotted an opportunity that I knew would benefit me, it was almost as if a light bulb went off in my head. You need to know what cues to look for when an opportunity comes your way. Most times it won't seem like there's even a benefit in it to begin with. But that's when you use your personal judgment.

My light bulb went off for me my freshmen year in college. Obviously, we go off to college to get good grades, an education, and most importantly, a full-time job by the time we graduate. At MSU and I'm sure just about every other college or university, they have career fairs. For those who may not know, career fairs are normally 1-3 day events where hundreds of companies/organizations come out and are looking to hire students for internships and/or full-time positions. While most companies are usually looking to hire juniors/seniors, I viewed this as an opportunity for me as a freshman to gain some insight and find out what separated a good candidate from a great candidate.

Light bulb moment: Well I knew that I would someday be a junior and a senior, so why not see what it was recruiters were looking for during my freshman year and then have two years to prepare myself for when it was my time to shine? So that is exactly what I did. I stumbled while talking to recruiters, learned what type of questions I should be asking, what recruiters were looking for, etc. I made sure I kept all of the business cards I received and followed-up and prepared myself two years in advance. "Every Day Is An Interview" at its finest, needless to say.

I then went again my sophomore year to learn even more new stuff! I would eavesdrop on the conversations other students would have with recruiters and say to myself "They probably won't get hired." based off of the responses they were given. I watched people come in there not in the correct dress code, etc. And I realized that they didn't prepare themselves in advance. Had they came to prior career fairs, they would have made those mistakes early on and would've made for a smoother and more successful career fair.

By the time my junior and senior years career fair had rolled around, I was overly prepared and ready for success! I was well-dressed, confident and knew just about every recruiter at the company I was interested in applying for. It allowed for a smooth conversation and a foot in – the – door to every single opportunity I wanted. That's how it should be. If the opportunity is there, make sure you take advantage of it! Even if it's not going to be able to get used until two to three years down the road, remember: YOU CAN NEVER BE TOO PREPARED FOR AN OPPORTUNITY.

I'll never forget this quote my middle school basketball coach gave us on a piece of paper as we left practice one day, **"It's best to be prepared for an opportunity and be able to pick and choose which one you would like to go after than to not be prepared at all and let an opportunity slip past you without you even noticing it." -Unknown**

The perfect example of always being prepared for an opportunity is one my former Sales Communication Professor, Jennifer Rumler, used to share with our class. "My students and I were in Rome on our study abroad program, "Made in Italy", and we were in a beautiful park called Villa Borghese practicing elevator pitches. I told the students that they needed to be as prepared as possible because you never know whom you will meet and how that may turn into a networking or career opportunity. One of the students told the group that she wanted to seek employment with the GAP. After our class session in the park, we left to go to the Joel Nafuma Refugee Center, a day center for political refugees from African and Middle Eastern countries, where we work three days a week as part of my Intercultural Communication and Sales course. There was a woman who was leading a group of high school students who also were working at the Center, and once introductions were made, we discovered that she was the VP of HR for the GAP. Not only did my student get to put her elevator pitch to good use, the woman asked her for her resume, which she had at her fingertips and gave it to her on the spot. Again, you never know whom you will meet or when your preparation will meet an opportunity; some people call it luck, I call luck the place where opportunity and preparation meet."

You see, preparation is key. You can't necessarily predict the future, but you can predict your tendencies to use strategic planning as a way to set yourself up for success in the long run. Not using strategic planning and failure to plan will lead to you planning to fail.

The GAP example is the perfect representation of "Every Day Is An Interview". If you practice good habits day in and day out, you'll never have to get ready because you'll already be ready!

KEY # 4

WALK BY FAITH,
NOT BY SIGHT

This relates to the first key in a way. Pretty much, it's all about YOU being proactive and taking that first initial step. Nobody is going to help you without you first helping yourself. Many people don't want to try something without being too sure of what the outcome or end result will be. Have you ever attempted something not too sure of what the end result was going to be? What was the end result?

Maybe it was trying a new recipe in the kitchen, or being the first one in your family to graduate from college? Was the end result greater than what you anticipated it on being? Now imagine if you never even attempted or tried that first step, how different could things have gone for you?

I've taken the initiative to make smart decisions on my life a plethora of times. A decision that I can recall being one that stood out was my decision to join the MSU Marketing Association my freshman year. In the beginning, everything aligned perfectly and made logical sense. I was looking to major in marketing, so I figured I might as well join the Marketing

Association to establish a large network and take advantage of every opportunity that presented itself.

I remember walking into the first meeting and being the only African American person in the room. As my hand neglected to turn loose the door handle, I stood there contemplating on if I wanted to leave or not. Something in me said just stay, so I did. Would you believe me if I told you I made the Executive Board my freshman year heading into my sophomore year, being one of two freshman to be even bold enough to apply for the position?

I connected with hundreds of students who had similar career interests as me and I leveraged their knowledge. I was an Executive Board member on the MSU Marketing Association from the end of my freshman year all the way to the last semester of my senior year. The benefit of being a member on the board was I had the opportunity to have direct access to our corporate sponsors and recruiters. I had the pleasure of knowing all of our direct recruiters' contact information, which set me up perfectly when it came time to get internships and full-time opportunities.

I often think back to that day when I almost turned around and walked out of that meeting. Have you ever opened a door and when you peeked your head in you didn't see what you thought you wanted to see so you turned around and walked out?

Behind every closed door that you open is not going to be what you expect. For it is up to you to decide if you're willing to make sacrifices early on so that the future can be a lot more gratifying than what you are currently experiencing. It is important that you lead on faith for understanding and not sight because faith can open up doors that your sight was too weak enough to even envision.

KEY #5

GET COMFORTABLE BEING UNCOMFORTABLE

> **Never get too comfortable, always challenge yourself.**
> **Comfort often times creates conditions for complacency.**
> **Go harder, dig deeper, push.**
>
> **—Unknown**

This applies to pretty much everything – whether it's your career, relationship, network, etc. Complacency should never be something you should be okay with. You should always want more out of something. I'm in sales so of course, I live and breathe this mentality, but the same rules should apply to you too!

Spiritually, you can never get too comfortable in your relationship with God. We must always be looking for ways to grow our relationship with the Lord. At times you may feel like you are in a good spot with the Lord just because you've been going to church consecutively for a few weeks and you suddenly began to get comfortable. You think you have room to relax. No! This is when you need to kick it in second gear and start taking extra steps. Maybe it's time to get one of your friends on the same relationship level with the Lord as you, etc.

One of the biggest mistakes people make is after a few good strides, they stop putting as much effort in because they think they have done enough to win. A perfect example of this was in Super Bowl 51, when the Atlanta Falcons had a 25 point lead over the New England Patriots. The Falcons thought they had the game in the bag and started to get comfortable.

> **Don't get too comfortable with who you are at any given time - you may miss the opportunity to become who you want to be.**
>
> **—Jon Bon Jovi**

What they didn't realize was that Tom Brady had a little bit more left in him. Instead of getting too comfortable and accepting the defeat that his team was facing, he dug deep down inside himself and overcame the situation and became the first quarterback and team to ever overcome such a deficit. The Atlanta Falcons were too busy watching the scoreboard and thinking about what had already happened in the past. "No team has ever come back after being down 20+ points." They thought they were all good. But what they found out was that when you get too comfortable you began to show a sign of weakness and it's that much easier for the enemy to spot it and capitalize on it.

Remember, the moment when you think you've gave it your all and have done enough to win is the moment where you need to do even more to weather the storm and come out on top. Fight until the very end. And when you feel like you can't go any longer, give it one last try.

KEY #6

KNOW YOUR WORTH

T hroughout this book, I share a lot of stories and experiences in which I remained persistent. No matter how gloomy the situation looked or how big the task was, I never got discouraged. I failed and even got knocked down a few times, but the key was that I consistently and unhesitantly got back up. You have to remember that when it comes to YOUR life and something YOU really want, YOU must stay true to yourself and the end result. If you want something, you have to go and get it! It's that simple. You cannot accept "NO" for an answer!

You ever wanted something so bad that you refuse to take "NO" for an answer? This was me. I've always been the type of person to go after my dreams, especially when they seemed unattainable or far-fetched. Growing up, all of my dreams scared me. Not having many positive role models to look up to, I always found myself having to "step out on faith" and lead not on my sight for answers but learn from my failures.

I met a guy when I was in high school and although I can't quite remember his name, I do vividly recall a story he shared with me on how he came to value his life on a day-to-day basis. He told me that he once had a heart attack. His health was perfectly fine and then one day all of a sudden, he woke up and his heart nearly gave up on him. From that point forward, he did not take his life for granted. He woke up every day with a sense of urgency because he knew that at any moment, his life could be taken away from him for good.

While it took him a near death experience to appreciate the beauty of life, for some, waking up with a purpose may come naturally to them. Regardless of what it takes you to go through to derive on a clear focus on life, they key is that you know your worth.

In life, it's imperative that you find a purpose. You literally have to look yourself in the mirror and say, "What is my purpose in life?" Having a purpose will allow for you to pursue your dream because you have an end goal. You have something to look forward to. Many fail at life because they have nothing to look forward to and they don't know what they are even looking for to begin with.

People wonder why their relationships fail – because they don't know what they want out of the relationship. Is it the thought of being in a relationship that people enjoy so much? Are they looking for someone to support them mentally, physically, financially?

Many fail at job searches. They don't know what they are looking for. They waste their time applying to random jobs, hoping to hear back instead of just narrowing down the job search to a specific focus or criteria. Are you looking for a high paying job? Is it the experience you want from the job? Is it the big name company you want to work for? Having a specific approach to a situation will create a much better ending because you know exactly how to identify an opportunity and how to correctly go after it.

Steve Harvey explains how to pursue your dreams.

"That is why people wake up in a rut.
There life has no purpose, no meaning.
There not "morning people". 'I'm just not a
morning person.'
You're not a morning person because….
you are not living in your purpose.
You hate waking up and you don't know the reason.
You're waking up and you don't have a design in mind.
Once you live in your purpose, when you discover your
gift, you can't wait to wake up!
Or at least when you wake up, you are happy
about waking up."

—Steve Harvey

This is the culture that "Every Day Is An Interview" promotes. When you begin to practice good habits everyday and stop taking shortcuts, being prepared becomes the norm. Stay woke people!

KEY # 7

DO YOU MEASURE UP?

> **Don't measure yourself by what you have accomplished, but by what you should have accomplished with your ability.**
> **—John Wooden**

The key in this quote is "What you should have accomplished". Since you can't change the past, you must let go of all of the frustration, anger and guilt that is stopping you from experiencing the present. Ask yourself, "Am I selling myself too short? Am I putting my best foot forward and being the best me that I can be every single day of my life? What am I learning from the challenges I'm facing in my life?" If you are going to reflect on the past, do it from a non-emotional state. You can't change any of it, so why waste your time and energy on it? It's just not worth it.

You wouldn't even know what you should have been able to do differently had you not lived through it with the choices you've already made. It's only having gone through the situation with the choices you made at the time, that you would even decide now that you would've done it differently, or if it was a so called "mistake". I'm not saying don't measure yourself; definitely measure yourself by what you have accomplished. But what's most important is that you ask yourself, "What can I be accomplishing now with the wisdom gained from the past and the growth that I experienced so that I can be better than I was before?"

Lesson on life: Looking back and wondering 'what went wrong' or 'why' will not change what happened. What you can change is what is happening now and the choices you make about the future. Life is not about being stuck in the past, it's about the experiences you currently have in the present and what you can do with them in the future.

The important thing is that we learn from the past, live for the present and hope for the future.

KEY #8

REFLECTION TIME

> "The only time you should ever look back
> is to see how far you've come."
> —Bangtan Boys, Butterfly

What is your look back and reflect moment? For me, it was foster care. Anytime I felt like giving up, I would think back to being in foster care, and how I wanted to give up and quit but I didn't, and look where I'm at today. I use my "look back" moments as motivation to keep me level headed.

Are you the type of person who plans for the worst or expect smooth sailing? Think about these two different approaches. If you are expecting smooth sailing, your effort will be very low and monotone because you have instilled in your mind that nothing is going to go wrong. Since you think that nothing is going to go wrong, you resist putting any effort in.

Those who expect smooth sailing are generally lazy people. Deep down inside, they know all potential outcomes that can happen in the event the situation happens to go wrong. However, they don't want to put the extra effort in upfront. Those who expect smooth sailing are typically procrastinators. They normally wait to the last (I mean very last) moment to decide to fix an already out of control situation.

If you are planning for the worst, there's always going to be some upside because you are never going to get too comfortable (Key #5). There shouldn't be any point in your life where you feel like you're too comfortable. Not being comfortable means you're always ready for an unexpected cause to happen. That's the biggest take away – you are prepared for war! You have the proper protocol and tools needed to be successful in any dangerous situation. Those who plan for the worst are highly trained and are process driven people. When the worst happens, they never overreact because they are already prepared to attack the situation.

Imagine if your flight attendant(s) were the type of people who expected smooth sailing. They didn't give you the safety message before takeoff on how to survive a plane crash in the event this unforeseen obstacle just so happened to take place. Do you know how many people will probably have lost their lives because of this?

This is not to say that if the flight attendant(s) had given the safety message that people still wouldn't have died, it's the simple fact that they would have at least knew how to react and potentially survive the catastrophic event.

All I'm saying is it's best to have a proactive plan in life instead of a reactive plan. Those who have a reactive approach when it comes to planning are the ones who fear the future.

They expect their current state to be this way forever. On the other hand, those who have a proactive approach when it comes to planning, have the ability to shape the future. In fact, they look forward to the future because they are confident in their abilities to control the outcome.

KEY #9

FRIENDS – HOW MANY OF US HAVE THEM?

> "If you're the smartest person in your group,
> then you need a new group."
> —Les Brown

You should only be surrounding yourself with those individuals who bring out the best in you.

Ask yourself the following questions:

- **Do my friends hold me accountable to certain goals or expectations that I have set for myself?**
- **Is my relationship with (insert close friend(s) name here) nurturing enough to the point that I'm a better person because I know (him/her)? Vice versa?**
- **Do my actions and efforts inspire not only my personal group of friends but others outside of my personal friend group?**

If you answered "NO" to any of the above questions then you need a new group of friends. A lot of times, we outgrow our friends for whatever reason and because we don't want to hurt their feelings, we tend to hold onto them as a common courtesy. It is okay to let them go! An easy way to let go of friends you outgrow is to think of that person as negative energy. Every time they come around you, imagine them extracting out your creative juices and abilities. It is imperative that you surround yourself with those who are going to inspire you to want more out of your own personal life.

Are you walking with the right group of people? A wise man once said "He who walks with the wise becomes wise." If you choose to surround yourself with those who are educated and knowledgeable, chances are their impact will rub off on you and you're going to realize that in order for you to remain a good fit for this group, you too, are going to have to put in some effort to rise up to the standards that has now been created.

On the other hand, if you surround yourself with fools, for lack of a better word, you are going to fall victim to their negative habits and ways, and eventually, you'll find yourself in a position where this daily routine also becomes habitual. You'll begin practicing bad habits and start taking shortcuts, which will eventually send you on the path you had no business being on in the first place.

We all know some really good people who made the mistake of deciding to clique up with the wrong friend group. Just one decision of selecting a wrong friend group can cause your life to make a turn for the worse.

To prevent this from happening in the first place, defriend anybody who doesn't live up to your personal standards on life.

KEY #10

CHOOSE THE ROAD LESS TRAVELED

Two roads diverged in a yellow wood
And sorry I could not travel both
And be one traveler, long I stood
And looked down one as far as I could
To where it bent in the undergrowth

Then took the other as just as fair
And having perhaps the better claim
Because it was grassy and wanted wear
Though as for that, the passing there
Had worn them really about the same

And both that morning equally lay
In leaves no step had trodden black
Oh, I kept the first for another day!
Yet, knowing how way leads onto way
I doubted if I should ever come back

> **I shall be telling this with a sigh**
> **Somewhere ages and ages hence**
> **Two roads diverged in a wood**
> **And I took the one less traveled by**
> **And that has made all the difference**
> **—Robert Frost**

I stumbled upon this poem in middle school and it seems to still be relevant today. While there is still a ton of confusion on what the true meaning of this poem was about, what I took away from it was how the writer stood in between two roads that appeared to be somewhat similar to one another. However, he made the conscious decision to take the pathway less traveled, and that seemed to have made a huge difference on the outcome of his life. It doesn't mean that because he took the road less traveled that it essentially was the best decision he could have made, but he decided to be different and not follow the crowd.

My takeaway was this was all about risk. Why take the route that many have already traveled and left their footprint on? You should take the road that nobody has been brave enough to take before and create your own footprint – your own journey. And once you've done that, show people the way. Let them know that while the beginning of the path may have had some trees and other obstacles, you were able to lead yourself into the light. And to close it off, the best part is that you can look back and learn from your mistakes so that the next time you know the correct journey to follow.

Or even better, if you went down the wrong path the first time, you will be able to now look back and reflect on some things you may have done differently if given another chance. The funny thing about life and its excursions is it gives us some "buy-in" to be able to perform a personal assessment once the trial/tribulation has taken its course.

Remember: Either you're in a tunnel, on your way out, or on your way in. The key though, is to keep walking a straight path and to never get distracted. Eventually, you will the see light.

Philippians 4:13
I can do all things through Christ, who strengthens me.

I wanted to share the quote below, which a friend of mine had in their email signature.

> **The road to success is not straight. There is a
> curve called Failure,
> a loop called Confusion, speed bumps called Friends,
> red lights called Enemies, caution lights called Family.
> You will have flats called Jobs. But, if you have a spare
> called
> Determination, an engine called Perseverance,
> insurance called Faith, a driver called Jesus,
> you will make it to a place called Success.
> (Author Unknown)**

As you can see, the journey to success is never an easy road. There's going to be multiple distractions that will get in your way and block you from reaching the finish line. The key to always remember however, is as long as you have the determination to outlast the unforeseen, you will eventually make it to the end of the road.

KEY #11

SET THE STICKY NOTE HIGH

> "Shoot for the moon. Even if you miss,
> you'll land among the stars."
> —Norman Vincent Peale

In my commencement speech at MSU, I opened it up by referencing an icebreaker one of my bosses had my co-workers and I participate in during a Staff Retreat. He handed us each two sticky notes and told us to go stand near an empty spot on the wall. He then said "With the first sticky note, I want you to jump up and place it as high on the wall as you possibly can reach."

So just like he instructed, we all leaped up with what we assumed was our greatest effort and placed the first sticky note on the wall. He then said "Now, with the second sticky note, I want you to place that one higher than the first one." This time, we used even greater efforts to get the second sticky note to be higher than the first. While some landed theirs lower than or exactly the same height as the first one, others, including me, were able to place the second sticky note higher than the first. My boss then said, "Wait a minute. Wait a minute. I thought I specifically said, place the first sticky note as HIGH as you possibly can reach? Why is the second one higher?"

This was probably one of the greatest exercises I had ever participated in. It had so much value in it. The main takeaway for me was that I was able to apply this small icebreaker to everyday life. Many people treat looking for jobs or even relationships, to name a few, as reference points. They don't tend to grasp their full capabilities until they have failed or don't necessarily get the results they were looking for the first time. However, if they had given their all in the initial attempt, who knows, a second attempt might not have even been needed.

The ultimate goal is to have extremely high expectations and dreams set out for yourself. The reason this is critical is because even if you fail to accomplish your goals, there's a pretty good chance you'll come close. And once you come close, you'll begin to see that what you thought was a long shot really is a piece of cake.

In life, unlike the icebreaker, you're only given one sticky note. Make sure that when you decide to use it, you give everything that is within you to set the sticky note as high as you possibly can reach.

KEY #12

EVERY DAY IS AN INTERVIEW

During my collegiate career, I had a famous saying I religiously practiced on a day-by-day basis. "Every day is an interview". I challenged myself to treat every day as if I had an interview to go to. I knew that this personal challenge would allow for me to be at the top of my game each and every day. Because I treated every day as if I had an interview to go to, I knew I needed to dress this way as well to compliment my favorite saying.

Now if you know me, then you know I love to dress up. I enjoy dressing up for 2 main reasons. 1) I have hopes of being a CEO, so I like to dress for the job I want to someday have. And 2) People tend to respect me more when I'm dressed up. Every time I'm in a suit, I've noticed that more people tend to greet me, hold the door open for me, and are typically a lot more personable than when I have street clothes on.

As a campus ambassador for Men's Wearhouse during my senior year at Michigan State, I had the opportunity of providing organizations on campus with knowledgeable tips on how to get the perfect look for their upcoming interviews and career fairs. I've received great feedback from those groups and just wanted to share with a larger audience.

THE BASICS

When it comes to building the foundation for your business wardrobe, you want to start off with 3 basic suit colors. You should purchase your suits in this specific order, preferably 1) Black 2) Navy or dark blue and 3) Gray. The reason you should start off with these three basic suit colors is because they are interchangeable. You can leverage your wardrobe by switching up your look by wearing black slacks with a gray suit jacket, gray slacks with a blue suit jacket, and so on and so forth. Instead of wearing a solid-colored suit, you can spice it up a little bit by mixing n' matching your suit separates.

SHOES

For interview or business purposes, I'd recommend lace-up leather shoes. Get your wardrobe started with a pair of black dress shoes. Once the black dress shoes have been purchased, go ahead and purchase a pair of brown lace-ups as well. Quick fashion tip: Brown dress shoes look fantastic with a black suit or navy suit. It gives your suit a lot more flavor, if you will, instead of your standard black dress shoes with a black suit look. Another quick fashion tip: loafers represent a casual look, so you should stray away from them for interview purposes.

DRESS SHIRT

There are two types of looks when it comes to dress shirts. You have your primary look and then you have your secondary look. For interviews, you always want to go with your primary dress shirt option, which is simply your basic white dress shirt. A white dress shirt provides one with a clean and crisp look. Now let's say you have more than one interview with a company – this is when it is okay for you to go with your secondary look. Your secondary look can either be a navy or blue shirt. For women, pink is also approved for a secondary look.

BELT

SHOES SHOULD ALWAYS MATCH THE COLOR OF YOUR BELT – NO EXCEPTIONS (black belt – black dress shoes, brown belt – brown dress shoes). Remember: It's the little things like this that matters the most when it comes to dressing for success!

TIE

For interview purposes, your tie should be very conservative (Solid color; if you choose to wear a striped tie, wear one with very minimal stripes). The reason you go with a conservative tie during an interview is because you don't want it to be distracting.

BOW TIES

I often get asked the question, "Can I wear a bow tie to my interview?" A lot of people would say no, I, however, beg to differ. Before I explain my reasoning behind this, you must first understand that wearing a bow tie to an interview is looked at as a BOLD and risky move. But for me, a bow tie fits my character and personality, so it worked out perfectly for me. I would wear a bow tie specifically if I knew I had a group interview. I knew that all of the other candidates would have on a standard tie, so I automatically knew it would make me stand out. And who wouldn't want to stand out at a job interview?! It's also a great conversation starter too! So the key to wearing a bow tie to an interview is to be able to back it up with both your character and resume!

THE MOST IMPORTANT TIP

Please make sure to get your suit tailored! I cannot stress this enough. Nothing says "hire me" more than a tailored suit. Very rarely will you walk into a store, try on a suit, and it fit perfectly. I'm a firm believer, if you look good then you feel good. And if you feel good, you are going to be more confident in yourself, which in turn will allow for you to be on you're "A" game throughout the interview. I'm not the best when it comes to math, but I do know the perfect formula for getting a job is - Tailored suit + confidence = Hired!

TAILORED TIPS

Coat shoulders – should be fitted close to the body but at the same time, comfortable to your personal liking.

Sleeves – should end where the wrist begins. Dress shirt cuffs should be exposed slightly. To get the dress shirt to be exposed, gently grab the end cuffs of your dress shirt and stretch your arms out to the side after the suit jacket is on. About .5-1' of your dress shirt should be showing where your suit jacket ends.

Pants – should be fit to your waist (not too high, not too low) and the length should end at the top of your shoes. You do not want your pants to be so long to the point where they are dragging on the ground when you walk. This could damage the material of your pants.

Suit jacket – remember, the bottom button on a suit should NEVER be buttoned. If you have on a 3-button suit jacket, only button the top two. If you have on a 2-button suit jacket, only button the top button. When you get into the room of your interview and sit down, make sure you unbutton all of your buttons on your suit jacket to increase your comfort level.

COMMON MISTAKE

You have your tailored suit, you are well-groomed, confidence is through the roof, etc. You're getting ready to head to the interview and you unknowingly make the biggest mistake of your life – well not the biggest mistake, but one that potentially could be detrimental to you not getting your dream job. YOU FORGET TO TAKE YOUR SUIT JACKET OFF BEFORE GETTING IN THE CAR.

This is extremely important – let me tell you why. If you drive around with your suit jacket on, when you get out of the car, your suit jacket will be wrinkled in the back. Now if you put this in the interviewer perspective, your back is the last thing they see on your way out the door. Ask yourself, do you want to be known as the interviewer that had the wrinkled suit? I didn't think so.

That's it! You now have all of the information needed to be "dangerous" when it comes to dressing for success! I hope that a lot of this was review, but that you also learned at least one thing or two that you didn't know prior to reading this.

Now that you are looking like the CEO of a Fortune 500 company, all you have to do now is nail the interview, get hired, and go get results!!!!! Good luck and remember, every day is an interview!

KEY #13

MENTORSHIP

'll close out this book with the reason I believe I've been able to be so successful in my life. My mentors have all kept me level-headed, gave me great advice, and all believed in me from day one. I personally recommend you have at least 2-3 mentors minimum! The beauty in a mentor-mentee relationship is that the benefits are mutual, if done the right way. I'll never forget one of mentors telling me how much he had learned from me and has been inspired by all of my accomplishments, when the whole time I was basing my success off of his feedback.

I took pride in doing everything my mentors said, "I wish I had done this when I was your age? Or "I wish I would've known.." I viewed this as an opportunity to be better than they were. Which for most, is what mentors want you to be anyway.

You can never have too many mentors. In fact, the more mentors you have, the better. You might have an educational mentor, a religious mentor, a mentor at work, etc. The beauty is that each person has a specific reason for being in your life. During my time at MSU, I had 6 mentors and while I talked to some more than others, I knew that if I needed something from anyone of them, they were only one call away. Mentorship is all about relationship building. The closer you become to your mentor and the more information you're willing to disclose to them, the greater the benefit!

When I met with my mentors we normally would have lunch or dinner and we would spend a great amount of time catching up, talking about any issues that I was currently going through, new opportunities I was thinking about seeking, and much more. Another benefit of having multiple mentors is you can ask them all the same thing to see what type of responses you get.

For example, if you happen to be stuck in between making a difficult decision, ask your mentors and see what they say. If you get the same responses then you can use their feedback as the indicator to keep going with your idea or to simply cut it loose.

At the end of the day, mentors main role is to guide you by giving you a critical assessment on ways to improve your skillset and capabilities. Some people may not need mentors. I used to think like this. I was already self-motivated and determined but once I had mentors who stood in my corner rooting me on, I became an even hungrier person destined for success. I originally got the spirit of motivation for the very reason I knew I didn't have the resources needed to be successful. And because of that, I always found myself making a way out of no way. But once my mentors came around, it simulated the process, as they were able to send me on a path that would've been much faster than the one I would've had to find on my own.

The most rewarding benefit of mentorship is when you're in a position to give back and be a mentor to someone else. A promise I made to my mentors is that I would definitely pay it forward and give back to someone in need. Currently, I'm a Big Brother in the Big Brother Big Sister program, where I mentor a 14 year old male.

My ultimate goal in life is to launch my own mentorship program, where I mentor males. My plan is to get them while they are freshmen in high school. I then plan on equipping them with all the tools and knowledge needed to be successful high school graduates and even greater men in college! I want to give them everything I didn't have growing up as a kid and be used a resource to help as many people as I can.

I want to make a difference in the world and be the change I want to see. I want "Every Day Is An Interview" to become a culture for these individuals. As long as I speak it into existence, I know that my dream will eventually come true!

CONCLUSION

If you didn't take anything away from this book, I hope you at least took away the importance of failure. You absolutely cannot be afraid to fail.

I view failure as a breath of fresh air! As weird as this may sound, failure is a chance for you to rebuild your life. What worst can happen to you at this point? You've reached rock bottom and the only place to go is up! If you don't fail, that means you are not trying new things in life. If you don't fail, it means you aren't taking risks.

The thing about failure is that it helps weed out the weak. A lot of people view failure as a bad thing. They think that because they failed, they'll always be a failure. They think that a failed task or mission today means a failed task or mission tomorrow.

This is where I will be the first to tell you failure is a great thing! Failure allows you to measure up and identify all of the reasons and opportunities as to why you failed. From that point, it's up to YOU to look at the situation with a critical eye and figure out, "What can I do better?" or "What could I have done better to succeed?" The moment you embrace your failure, is the moment where you'll no longer accept defeat. The moment you embrace your failure, is the moment where losing becomes the new "winning".

You have to grab hold of your life and take 100% accountability for it. You should always be in competition with yourself! If you failed in doing something that you know for a fact you could've achieved, you need to go back to the drawing board and reevaluate both you and the situation. Were you not prepared? Did you overlook something?

I've found life's greatest rewards tend to be the one that were the toughest to achieve. Life's greatest rewards has been the ones that forced me outside of my comfort zone. When placed in positions I had no clue of how I would overcome, motivated me even more to find a way out of no way. That's the beauty of failure!

Every Day Is An Interview is all about failure. It's about how can I use everything that was set out against me to fail, whether that is certain people, experiences, etc., and in return, be able to breakthrough and overcome. It's about learning about yourself and understanding what are some things you need to work on to make you a better person tomorrow than you are today. It's about being able to look yourself in the mirror and able to honestly say that if today was my last day on earth, I would be proud of the person I am.

Preparation is the key. If you are not ready, now is the time to get ready! Every day is an interview.

CLOSING PRAYER

Dear Heavenly Father,

Thank you for giving me the strength, wisdom and knowledge to complete my first book. The ride has been wonderful. On this journey, I learned a lot about myself and my family history that I didn't know about before embarking on this journey. While I would like to think that this is the end, this is the beginning. Father God, I ask that this book will be the beginning to something special. I ask that you will bless those who have read this book and that you give them the strength to continue fighting whatever it is they are going through right now. Please cleanse their mind from any negative thoughts that are telling them that they can't do something. Create in them a renewed mind, ensuring them that they can do whatever it is that they put their mind to. In Jesus name I pray. Amen.